Push and Pull

Kaitlyn Duling

Rourke
Educational Media

A Division of
Carson
Dellosa
Education®

rourkeeducationalmedia.com

Before Reading: *Building Background Knowledge and Vocabulary*

Building background knowledge can help children process new information and build upon what they already know. Before reading a book, it is important to tap into what children already know about the topic. This will help them develop their vocabulary and increase their reading comprehension.

Questions and Activities to Build Background Knowledge:

1. Look at the front cover of the book and read the title. What do you think this book will be about?
2. What do you already know about this topic?
3. Take a book walk and skim the pages. Look at the table of contents, photographs, captions, and bold words. Did these text features give you any information or predictions about what you will read in this book?

Vocabulary: *Vocabulary Is Key to Reading Comprehension*

Use the following directions to prompt a conversation about each word.

- Read the vocabulary words.
- What comes to mind when you see each word?
- What do you think each word means?

Vocabulary Words:
- *direction*
- *energy*
- *force*
- *motion*

During Reading: *Reading for Meaning and Understanding*

To achieve deep comprehension of a book, children are encouraged to use close reading strategies. During reading, it is important to have children stop and make connections. These connections result in deeper analysis and understanding of a book.

 Close Reading a Text

During reading, have children stop and talk about the following:

- Any confusing parts
- Any unknown words
- Text to text, text to self, text to world connections
- The main idea in each chapter or heading

Encourage children to use context clues to determine the meaning of any unknown words. These strategies will help children learn to analyze the text more thoroughly as they read.

When you are finished reading this book, turn to the last page for an **After Reading Activity**.

Table of Contents

Let's Move

All living things need **energy** to move.

Our bodies get energy from the food we eat.

Plants get energy from the sun.

An object is not a living thing.

It needs a **force** applied to make it move.

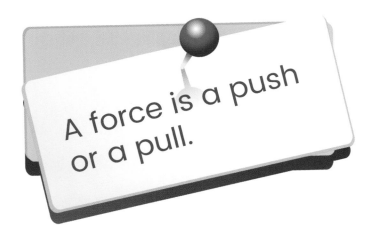
A force is a push or a pull.

8

Push and Pull

The merry-go-round is stopped.

We can use energy to make it move.

How? We push. The harder we push, the faster it goes.

We stop pushing. The merry-go-round slows and stops.

I push the truck. It moves forward.

I can pull it back too.

Changing Directions

I push and pull the wheelbarrow. When it is empty, it is easy.

Now it is full. I have to push hard.

I push the ball. It rolls to my friend.

She pushes the ball. It changes **direction**. It rolls back to me.

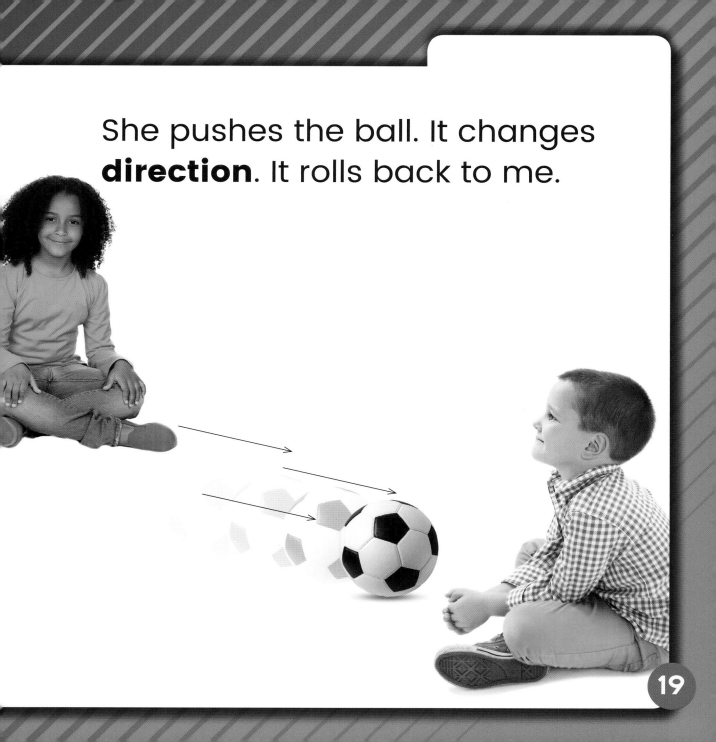

Pushes and pulls put objects in **motion**!

Photo Glossary

direction (duh-REK-shuhn): The path in which someone or something is moving or pointing.

energy (EN-ur-jee): The ability of something to do work

force (fors): Any action that changes the shape or the movement of an object.

motion (MOH-shuhn): Movement.

Marshmallow Shooter

Use force to make a marshmallow fly!

Supplies

paper or foam cup   mini marshmallows

balloon   ruler or measuring tape

scissors

Directions

1. With the help of an adult, cut the bottom out of a paper or foam cup.
2. Tie the bottom of a deflated balloon.
3. Cut the top off the balloon.
4. Stretch the top of the cut balloon across the bottom of the cup.
5. Put a mini marshmallow inside the cup. When you pull the balloon back, the force of air will push the marshmallow into motion.
6. Use a ruler or measuring tape to see how far the marshmallow flew.

Index

About the Author

Kaitlyn Duling is an avid reader and writer who grew up in Illinois. She now resides in Washington, D.C. Kaitlyn has written over 60 books for children and teens. You can learn more about her at www.kaitlynduling.com.

After Reading Activity

Put a cotton ball on the floor in front of you. How can you apply force to make it move? Can you push or pull it without your hands? Try to think of the fastest way to move the cotton ball from one side of the room to the other. Then challenge a friend to a race!

Library of Congress PCN Data

Push and Pull / Kaitlyn Duling
(My Physical Science Library)
ISBN 978-1-73161-409-4 (hard cover)(alk. paper)
ISBN 978-1-73161-204-5 (soft cover)
ISBN 978-1-73161-514-5 (e-Book)
ISBN 978-1-73161-619-7 (e-Pub)
Library of Congress Control Number: 2019932056

Rourke Educational Media
Printed in the United States of America,
North Mankato, Minnesota

www.rourkeeducationalmedia.com

Edited by: Kim Thompson
Produced by Blue Door Education for Rourke Educational Media.
Cover and interior design by: Nicola Stratford
Photo Credits: Cover logo: frog © Eric Phol, test tube © Sergey Lazarev, cover tab art © siridhata, cover photo © juninatt, cover title art © Vitaliy belozerov, page background art © Zaie; Page 4 © Rawpixel.com, Page 5 © Bildagentur Zoonar GmbH; page 6 © Black-Photogaphy, page 7 © lovelyday12, page 8 pushpin art © MilaLiu, page 9 © Daniel M. Nagy; page 10,11, 12, 13 © Oleg Mikhaylov; pages 14 and 15 © bigjom jom; page 16 and 16 © CroMary; page 18 and 19 boy © Jeka, girl © Gelpi, ball © FocusStocker; page 20 © Vinne All images from Shutterstock.com